PRAYER

I am going to strive to be productive for as long as I can.

I am going to make every day and every activity as precious and enjoyable as possible.

I am going to strive to be as gracious, warm, and charitable as possible.

I am going to strive to be healthy as long as I can.

I am going to strive to accept others' love in a deeper way than I have up to now.

I am going to strive to live a more fully "reconciled" life. No room for past hurts anymore.

I am going to strive to keep my sense of humor intact.

I am going to strive to be as courageous and brave as I can.

I am going to strive, always, to never look on what I am losing but rather to look at how wonderful and full my life has been and is.

And I am going to, daily, lay all of this at God's feet through prayer. Amen.

Getting in Touch with Our Longing

First Sunday of Advent

The days are coming, oracle of the LORD, when I will fulfill the promise I made to the house of Israel and the house of Judah. In those days, in that time, I will make a just shoot spring up for David.

JEREMIAH 33:14–15

Every Tear Brings the Messiah Closer

"People are always impatient, but God is never in a hurry!" Those words, written by Greek author Nikos Kazantzakis, highlight that we need to be patient, infinitely patient, with God.

Looking at religious history, we cannot help but be struck by the fact that God seemingly takes his time in the face of our impatience. Humanity's scriptures are often a record of frustrated desire and of human impatience.

We see in the Bible the constant, painful cry: *Come, Lord, come! Save us! How much longer must we wait? When, Lord, when?* We are forever impatient, but God refuses to be hurried. Why? Why is God seemingly so slow to act?

There's a line in Jewish apocalyptic literature that helps answer that question: Every tear brings the messiah closer! There is, it would seem, an intrinsic connection between frustration and the possibility of a messiah being born. It seems that messiahs can only be born after a long period of human yearning. Why?

Human birth helps answer that question. Gestation cannot be hurried, and there's an organic connection between the pain a mother experiences in childbirth and the delivery of a new life. That's also true of Jesus' birth. Advent is a gestation process that cannot be rushed. Tears, pain, and a long season of prayer are needed to create the conditions for the kind of pregnancy that brings forth a messiah into our world. Why? Because real love and life can only be born when

DAYbreaks

Daily Reflections for Advent and Christmas

RON ROLHEISER, OMI

DAYbreaks

Imprimi Potest: Stephen T. Rehrauer, CSsR, Provincial,
Denver Province, the Redemptorists

Published by Liguori Publications, Liguori, Missouri 63057.
To order, call 800-325-9521, or visit Liguori.org.

ISBN: 978-0-7648-2819-5

Liguori Publications, a nonprofit corporation, is an apostolate of the Redemptorists.
To learn more about the Redemptorists, visit Redemptorists.com.

Cover image: iStock
Interior Images: Shutterstock

Printed in the United States of America • First Edition
23 22 21 20 19 / 5 4 3 2 1

patience has created the correct space, a virginal womb within which the sublime can be born. Perhaps a metaphor would help.

John of the Cross, in explaining how a person comes to be enflamed in altruistic love, uses the image of a log bursting into flame in a fireplace. When a green log is placed in a fire, it doesn't start to burn immediately. It first needs to dry out. For a long time, it lies in the fire and sizzles, its greenness and dampness slowly getting drier. Only when it reaches kindling temperature can it ignite and burst into flame. So, too, with how real love is born in our lives. We ignite into love only when we—selfish, green, damp logs—have "sizzled" sufficiently. The fire that makes us sizzle is unfulfilled desire.

God is never in a hurry, and for good reason. Messiahs can only be born when there's enough patience to let things happen on God's terms, not ours.

Every tear should bring the Messiah closer: Every frustration should make us more open to love. Every tear should make us more ready to forgive. Every heartache should make us more ready to let go of some of our selfishness. Every unfulfilled ache should lead us into a more sincere prayer. All of our impatience should make us feverish enough to burst into love's flame.

It is with much groaning of the flesh that the life of the spirit is brought forth!

Messiahs can only be born after a long period of human yearning.

Monday
FIRST WEEK OF ADVENT

Learning How to Wait

Carlo Carretto spent many years living as a hermit in the Sahara Desert. From that place of solitude he was asked if he had a message for the world. "What do you hear God trying to tell us?" someone asked him. His answer: "God is saying: Be patient! Learn to wait! Learn to wait for each other, for love, for happiness, for God!" Learn to wait! That's not something we do easily, and many of our problems flow from that missing piece. We often don't wait properly for things.

Annie Dillard shares this story about proper waiting: She had been watching a butterfly emerge from its cocoon and was fascinated by the process until she grew impatient with how long it was taking and, to speed things up, took a candle and heated the cocoon, albeit very gently. The butterfly then emerged more quickly; however, because adding heat violated something within the natural process, the butterfly was born with wings too weak to fly. Haste and prematurity had stunted and deformed a natural process.

Some things can't be rushed. Impatience often triggers an irreverence that damages the natural order of things. In essence, the Christmas gift is opened too early; the bride is slept with before the wedding; a process that needs an allotted period of time is short-circuited. There isn't enough Advent.

Advent means waiting. For something sublime to be born, there must first be a proper time of waiting, a season of patience. Advent is an invitation to patience.

God wants us to learn "to wait for each other, for love, for happiness, for God!"

CARLO CARRETTO, WHO LIVED AS A HERMIT

Tuesday
FIRST WEEK OF ADVENT

Raising Our Psychic Temperature

Pierre Teilhard de Chardin once suggested that we will come to community with each other when we reach a high enough psychic temperature so as to burn away the things that still hold us apart. He was drawing upon a principle in chemistry where sometimes two elements will simply lie side by side inside a test tube and not unite until sufficient heat is applied so as to bring them to a high enough temperature where unity can take place.

That's a wonderful Advent metaphor. Advent is about letting our yearnings raise our psychic temperatures so we're pushed to eventually let down our guard, hope in new ways, and risk intimacy.

How do we raise our psychic temperature? I believe we do so by letting the pain of loneliness, restlessness, disquiet, anxiety, frustration, and unrequited desire stretch our souls so that we open ourselves to community in new ways.

Scripture tells us that the kingdom of God is not a matter of eating and drinking, of simple bodily pleasure, but a coming together in justice, peace, and joy in the Holy Spirit. Ultimately, that is what we ache for in our loneliness and longing: consummation, oneness, intimacy, completeness, harmony, peace, and justice.

Advent is about heightening our longing, about letting it raise our psychic temperatures, about sizzling as damp, green logs inside the fires of frustration, about intuiting through desire what the world might look like if a messiah were to come and, with us, establish justice, peace, and unity on this earth.

The kingdom of God is a coming together in the Holy Spirit.

Wednesday
FIRST WEEK OF ADVENT

Inchoate Desire

My soul longs for you in the night. For you alone do I thirst!

BASED ON PSALM 63:2

A lot of times, we long for things that are not of God. How often can we honestly pray: "For you, God, alone do I long," when we long for many things that aren't God-focused at all.

Desire is complex. There's surface desire and there's deep desire, and in every one of our longings and motivations we can ask: *What am I really looking for here? I know what I want on the surface, here and now, but what am I ultimately longing for?*

Imagine this: A man—lonely, restless, and depressed—goes to a singles' bar and picks up a prostitute. On the surface his motivation and desire are as undisguised as they are crass. He's not longing for God in this particular act. Or is he?

On the surface, of course, he's not. His desire is purely self-centered, not God-centered. But at a place deep inside him, he's longing for divine intimacy, for the bread of life. But he isn't aware of this because, on this given night, something else is promising him a more immediate tonic.

Yes, our lives are marked by flirtations and encounters that exhibit desires that are seemingly not for the bread of life. But they are, and Advent asks us to contemplate their true consummation.

At a place deep inside, we long for divine intimacy.

Living with Longing

Today we struggle to carry tension for long periods of time, to live with frustration, to accept incompleteness, to be at peace with the circumstances of our lives, to be comfortable inside our own skins, and to live without consummation in the face of sexual desire. Of course, in the end, we do not have a choice. We are not above our humanity and simply have to accept and live with the tensions of incompleteness, but we need to do so without bitter impatience, pathological restlessness, and all kinds of compensatory activities.

Emotionally and morally, this is our Achilles' heel. Today's people have some wonderful emotional and moral qualities, but patience, chastity, contentment with the limits of circumstance, and the capacity to nobly live out tension are not our strengths.

And the fault is not entirely our own. Too many of us were never taught that life is hard, that we have to spend most of it waiting in one kind of frustration or other, and that this is the natural state of things.

Most of us will have to learn this the hard way, through bitter experience, through tears, and through a lot of restlessness from which we might be spared if we already knew that hunger, not satiation, is what is normal. To paraphrase a statement by Karl Rahner: In the torment of the insufficiency of everything attainable we finally learn that here in this life all symphonies must remain unfinished.

Many were never taught that waiting in frustration is normal.

Friday
FIRST WEEK OF ADVENT

In Our Daydreams, We Intuit the Kingdom

We daydream a lot, though few will admit it. We're all
pathological daydreamers, and that isn't necessarily bad. Our hearts and
minds, chronically frustrated by the limits of our lives, naturally seek
solace in daydreaming. It's an irresistible temptation. Hence the escape
into daydreams. And what are the contents of those daydreams?

In our daydreams, we create fantasy lives for ourselves that we play
over and over again in our minds as we might play and replay a favorite
movie. But there's something important to note here. In our daydreams,
we're never petty or small. We're always noble and grand, the hero/
heroine, generous, bighearted, immune from faults, drawing perfect
respect, and making perfect love. In our daydreams we, in fact, intuit
the vision of Isaiah where he foresees a perfect world, the lamb and the
lion lying down together, the sick being healed, the hungry being fed,
all restlessness being brought to calm, and God drying every tear. Isaiah
also fantasied about perfect consummation. His fantasy was a prophecy.
In our earthy fantasies, we intuit the kingdom of God.

Of course, this has a downside: Since in our daydreams we're always
the center of attention and admiration, our daydreams can easily stoke
our natural narcissism. But, as Henri Nouwen suggests, one of the
important struggles in our lives is to turn our fantasies into prayer.
That's the task of Advent.

In our daydreams, we're never petty or small.
We're always noble and grand.

Saturday
FIRST WEEK OF ADVENT

Lighting an Advent Candle, Giving Hope

In the days of apartheid in South Africa, Christians were accustomed to lighting candles and placing them in windows as a sign to themselves and others that they believed someday this injustice would end. A candle burning in a window was a sign of hope. The government understood the message and passed a law making it illegal to place a lit candle in a window, an offense equal to owning a firearm. Both were considered equally dangerous. This eventually became a joke among the kids: "Our government is afraid of lit candles!"

For good reason. Lit candles, more than firearms, overthrew apartheid. Hope, not guns, ultimately transforms things. To light a candle as an act of hope is to say to yourself and to others that, despite anything that might be happening in the world, you are still nursing a vision of peace and unity based upon something beyond the present state of things.

We light Advent candles with that in mind, accepting that the evening news will not always be positive, that the stock markets will not always rise, that the most sophisticated defenses in the world will not always protect us from terrorism.

We light candles in hope because we believe that God, who is more real than anything else, has promised to establish a kingdom of love and peace on this earth and is gracious, forgiving, and powerful enough to do so.

We know the evening news won't always be good, but we light a candle anyway.

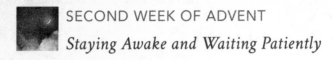

Staying Awake and Waiting Patiently

Second Sunday of Advent

And do this because you know the time; it is the hour now for you to awake from sleep. For our salvation is nearer now than when we first believed.

ROMANS 13:11

Staying Awake

In his autobiography, *Report to Greco*, Greek philosopher and writer Nikos Kazantzakis recounts a conversation he once had with an old monk. Kazantzakis, a young man at the time, was visiting a monastery and was very taken by a famed ascetic who lived there, Fr. Makarios, and asked him for some spiritual advice. The old monk said simply: "Wake up, my child. Wake up before death wakes you up."

Jesus is always telling us to wake up, to stay awake, to be vigilant. What does he mean by that? How are we asleep?

All of us know how difficult it is for us to be inside the present moment, to not be asleep to the real riches inside our own lives. The distractions and worries of daily life tend to so consume us that we habitually take for granted what's most precious to us: our health, the miracle of our senses, the love and friendships that surround us, and the gift of life itself. We go through our daily lives not only with a lack of reflectiveness and gratitude but often with a habitual touch of resentment as well, a chronic, gray depression. We are very much asleep, both to God and to our own lives.

How do we wake up? Today there's a rich literature that offers us all kinds of advice on how to get into the present moment so we can be awake to the deep riches inside our own lives. While much of this literature is good, little of it is very effective. It invites us to live each day of our lives as if it were our last day, but we simply can't do that. It's impossible to sustain that kind of intentionality and awareness over a long time. An awareness of our mortality does wake us up—a stroke, a heart attack, or cancer—but that heightened awareness is easier to sustain for a short season of our lives than it is for twenty, thirty, forty, or fifty years. Nobody can sustain that kind of awareness all the time. Or can we?

Spiritual wisdom offers a nuanced answer: We can and we can't! On the one hand, the distractions, cares, and pressures of everyday life will invariably have their way with us and we will, in effect, fall asleep to what's deeper and more important inside of life. But it's for this reason that every major spiritual tradition has daily rituals designed precisely to wake us from spiritual sleep, akin to an alarm clock waking us from physical sleep.

None of us lives each day as if it were his or her last. Our heartaches, headaches, distractions, and busyness invariably lull us to sleep. That's forgivable; it's what it means to be human. So it's important that we make sure we have regular spiritual rituals, prayer, and Eucharist to jolt us back awake—so that it doesn't take a heart attack, a stroke, cancer—or death—to wake us up.

*We are very much asleep,
both to God and to our own lives.*

Monday
SECOND WEEK OF ADVENT

Patience with God

There's an adage that says an atheist is someone who can't grasp metaphor. Thomas Halik, the Czech writer, would instead suggest that an atheist is someone who can't be patient enough with God.

There's a lot of truth in that. Patience with God is perhaps our greatest faith struggle. God, it would seem, is never in a hurry and because of that we live with an impatience that can test the strongest faith and the stoutest heart.

We want a God who rescues us, who intervenes actively for justice and goodness in this world, who acts visibly now in this life, and who doesn't let us get sick and die. No one wants a God who asks us to live in a lifelong patience predicated on the promise that, in the end (whenever that will be), love and justice will prevail, all tears will be dried, and all will finally be well.

Why the need for such great patience? Does God want to test us? Does God want to see if we truly have a faith that is worthy of a great reward? No. God has no need to play such a game.

The need for patience arises from the rhythms innate within life itself and within love itself. They need to unfold, as do flowers and pregnancies, according to their own inherent rhythms and within their own good time. They can't be rushed, no matter how great our impatience or how great our discomfort.

We live with an impatience that can test the strongest faith and the stoutest heart.

Tuesday
SECOND WEEK OF ADVENT

The Sublime and Sublimation

Celebration is a paradoxical thing, created by a dynamic interplay between anticipation and fulfillment, longing and consummation, the ordinary and the special, work and play.

We struggle with this today. Many of our feasts fall flat because there hasn't been a previous fast. In times past, there was generally a long fast leading up to a feast, and then a joyous celebration followed. Today we've reversed that. There is a long celebration leading up to the feast and a fast afterward.

Take Christmas, for example. In modern times, the season of Advent, in essence, kicks off the Christmas celebration. The parties start, the decorations and lights go up, and the Christmas music begins to play. When Christmas finally arrives, we're already satiated with the delights of the season, tired, ready to move on. By Christmas Day, we're ready to go back to ordinary life. The Christmas season used to last until February. Now, realistically, it's over on December 25.

We are poorer for that. Without a previous fast, there isn't much sublimity in the feast. In short, Christmas is no longer special because we've celebrated it during Advent. Weddings are no longer special because we've already slept with the bride. And experiences of all kinds are often dull and unable to excite us because we had them prematurely.

It's Advent. If we use this season to fast, to intensify longing, and to raise our psychic temperatures, then the feast that follows will have a chance to be sublime.

Let's live Advent the right way.

Wednesday
SECOND WEEK OF ADVENT

Mourning Our Barrenness

Barrenness is not just a term that describes a biological incapacity to have children or a choice not to have them. It's more. Barrenness describes the universal human condition in its incapacity to be generative in the way it would like and the vacuum and frustration that remains in our lives.

Karl Rahner summarizes that in these words: "In the torment of the insufficiency of everything attainable, we ultimately learn that here, in this life, all symphonies must remain unfinished." No person has a finished symphony here on earth. There's always some barrenness that remains in our lives, and biological barrenness is simply one example of that—though arguably the prime one. No one dies having "given birth" to all she or he wanted to in this world.

What do we do in the face of this emptiness? Is there a response that can take us beyond simply gritting our teeth and stoically getting on with it?

There is. The answer is tears. In midlife and beyond, we need, as Alice Miller normatively suggests in her classic essay *The Drama of the Gifted Child* to mourn so that our very foundations are shaken.

Many of our wounds are irreversible and many of our shortcomings are permanent. We will go to our deaths with this incompleteness. Our loss cannot be reversed. But it can be mourned, both what we lost and what we failed to achieve. In that mourning there is freedom.

None of us has a finished symphony on earth, but there is freedom beyond the pain.

Thursday
SECOND WEEK OF ADVENT

Patience Requires Perseverance

There is a Norwegian proverb that reads: "Heroism consists of hanging on one minute longer." When I was a child, one of the stories in a school textbook had that title. It told of a young boy who had fallen through the ice while skating and was left clinging, cold and alone, to the edge of the ice with no help in sight. As he hung on in this seemingly hopeless situation, he was tempted many times to simply let go since no one was going to come along to rescue him. But he held on, despite all odds. Finally, when everything seemed beyond hope, he clung on one minute longer and, after that extra minute, help arrived.

The story is simple and its moral is simple: This young boy lived because he had the courage and strength to hang on one minute longer. Rescue comes just after you have given up on it, so extend your courage and wait one minute longer.

This is a tale of physical heroism and makes its point clearly. Heroism often consists in staying the course long enough, of hanging on when it seems hopeless, of suffering cold and aloneness while waiting for a new day.

Scripture teaches much the same thing about moral heroism. In Galatians 6:9, St. Paul may well have inspired that Norwegian proverb when he writes: "Let us not grow tired of doing good, for in due time we shall reap our harvest, if we do not give up."

If the fight has value, keep hanging on.

Friday
SECOND WEEK OF ADVENT

The Arrival of the Kingdom

Most of us are well-intentioned, but we push the things we need to change in our lives off into the future: *Yes, I need to do this, but I'm not ready yet. I want more time. Sometime in the future I'll do this.*

When Jesus says he has come to bring us new life, he is not talking simply about our future lives in heaven. He is also talking about our lives here, now. The new life is already here, he assures us.

Jesus preached this very clearly, and the problem was not that his hearers didn't understand him. They understood. But, almost universally, they resisted that message. Having God become concrete in their lives was far too threatening.

We're like the guests in the Gospel parable who are invited to a wedding banquet. We also want to go to the feast. We intend to go to the feast. But first we need to attend to our marriages, our businesses, our ambitions. We can get serious later.

You may be familiar with the infamous prayer of St. Augustine. If not, I suggest you look it up. After converting to Christianity at age twenty-five, he struggled for another nine years to bring his sexuality into harmony with his faith. Sometime during those nine years, he asked God to "grant me chastity...but not yet." To his credit, unlike many people, at least he eventually stopped pushing things into the indefinite future.

Heaven is here.

Is having God as a force in our lives too threatening?

God's Quiet Presence

The poet Rumi submits that we live with a deep secret that sometimes we know, and then not. That concept can be helpful in understanding our faith. One reason we struggle with faith is that God's presence inside us and in our world is rarely dramatic, overwhelming, sensational, something impossible to ignore. God doesn't work like that. Rather, God's presence—much to our frustration and loss of patience sometimes—is something that lies quiet and seemingly helpless inside us. It rarely makes a huge splash.

Because we are not sufficiently aware of this, we tend to misunderstand the dynamics of faith and find ourselves habitually trying to ground our faith on precisely something that is loud and dramatic. We are forever looking for something beyond the gifts God gives us.

But we can learn from the very way God was born into our world that faith needs to ground itself on something that is quiet and undramatic. Jesus, as we know, was born into our world with no fanfare and no power, a baby helpless in the straw, another child among millions. The God that Jesus incarnates is neither dramatic nor splashy.

This is important for understanding faith. God lies inside us as an invitation that fully respects our freedom, never overpowering us. God also never goes away. God-as-invitation lies there precisely like a baby in the straw, gently beckoning us but helpless. God can't make us pick up and accept his invitation.

God lies like a baby in the straw, gently beckoning us but helpless.

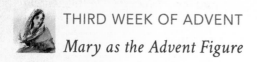

Mary as the Advent Figure

Third Sunday of Advent

And Mary said: "My soul proclaims the greatness of the Lord;
my spirit rejoices in God my savior."

LUKE 1:46–47

The Virgin Birth

Christian tradition has always emphasized that Jesus was born
of a virgin. The Messiah could only come forth from a virgin's womb.
The main reason for this emphasis, of course, is to highlight that Jesus
did not have a human father and that his conception was from the Holy
Spirit.

But there is often a secondary emphasis as well, less founded in
Scripture. Too common is the idea that Jesus was born from a virgin
because somehow sexuality is impure, that it is too base and earthy
to have a connection to such a sacred event. The holy must be kept
separate from what is base. Jesus wasn't just born of a virgin because he
did not have a human father; he was also born of a virgin because his
birth demanded a purity that, by definition, rules out sex. Our concept
of the virgin birth has been infiltrated by a piety which, for all kinds of
reasons, cannot accord sexuality to the holy.

What's wrong with this? Beyond denigrating the God-given
goodness of sexuality, it misses one of the major aspects of revelation
within the virgin birth. There is a moral challenge within the virgin
birth, something that invites imitation rather than admiration.

Christian tradition emphasizes a virgin birth (just as it emphasizes
a virgin burial, a virgin tomb to parallel the virgin womb) not because
it judges that sexuality is too impure and earthy to produce something
holy. Rather, beyond wanting to stress that Jesus had no human father,
the Christian tradition wants to emphasize what kind of heart and
soul is needed to create the space wherein something the divine can be
born. What is at issue is not celibacy rather than sex, but patience rather

than impatience, reverence rather than irreverence, respect rather than disrespect, and accepting to live in tension rather than capitulating and compensating in the face of unrequited desire.

A virgin's heart lets love unfold according to its own dictates rather than manipulating it. A virgin's heart lets gift be gift rather than somehow, however subtly, possessing it. A virgin's heart accepts the pain of inconsummation rather than sleeping with the groom before the wedding. That, in the end, is what constitutes virginal space, the space within which God can be born.

Why a virgin's womb for a messiah's birth? Why a focus on purity within the Christian tradition? Because, as we all know well, our lives are full of most everything that is not virginal or pure: impatience, disrespect, irreverence, manipulation, cynicism, grandiosity. And, as we also know, within this matrix no messiah can be gestated. The Messiah, the Christ, can only be born from a virgin's womb.

A virgin's heart
lets love unfold.
It lets gift be gift.

Monday
THIRD WEEK OF ADVENT

The Mary of the Gospels

In the synoptic Gospels, Mary is presented as a model of discipleship. But that isn't immediately evident. On the surface, the opposite sometimes seems to be the case.

For example, on a couple of occasions as Jesus is speaking to a crowd, he is interrupted and told that his mother and his family are outside wanting to speak to him. His response? "Who is my mother? Who are my brothers?....Whoever does the will of my heavenly Father is my brother, and sister, and mother."

In saying this, Jesus isn't distancing his mother from himself and his message. Rather, Jesus is singling out his mother first of all for her faith, not for her biology. She's the first to hear the word of God and keep it.

John's Gospel gives her a different role. Here she is presented as Eve, the mother of humanity, and the mother of each of us. Interestingly, John never gives us Mary's name. In the Gospel of John, Mary is always referred to as the Mother of Jesus.

As Eve, as universal mother, and as our mother, Mary stands in helplessness under human pain. When she stands under the cross, she is in human pain. In this, she shows herself as universal mother but also as an example of how injustice must be handled: namely, by standing within it in a way that doesn't replicate its hatred and violence so as to give it back in kind. Mary offers us a wonderful example, not to be ignored.

Mary is the first to hear the word of God and keep it.

Tuesday
THIRD WEEK OF ADVENT

Mary and a Chaste Goddess

Ancient Greece expressed much of its psychological and spiritual wisdom inside its myths. The Greeks didn't intend these to be taken literally or as historical but as metaphor and as archetypal illustrations. Many Greek myths are centered on gods and goddesses who mirrored virtually every aspect of life, every aspect of human behavior, and every innate human propensity.

There was a particular goddess name Artemis. Unlike most of the other goddesses, who were sexually promiscuous, she was chaste and celibate. She was pictured as a tall, graceful figure, attractive sexually but with a beauty that was different from the seductive sexuality of goddesses like Aphrodite and Hera.

Artemis represents a chaste way of being sexual. She tells us that, in the midst of a sexually soaked world, one can be generative and happy inside of chastity and even inside celibacy. Perhaps even more importantly, Artemis shows us that chastity need not render one anti-sexual and sterile.

What's taught by this mythical goddess is a much-needed lesson for our world today. Our age has turned sex into a soteriology. Specifically, for us, sex isn't perceived as a means toward heaven. It's identified with heaven itself. It's what we're supposed live for.

We're psychologically and spiritually impoverished by that notion, and it puts undue pressure on our sexual lives. When sex is asked to carry the primary load in terms of human generativity and happiness, it can't help but come up short.

If Artemis had been real and lived in the time of the Blessed Mother, the Virgin Mary would have been good friends with her.

A Greek goddess teaches a valuable lesson.

Mary's Partner in Giving Christ to Us: Joseph

Who is Joseph? He's that quiet figure prominently named in the Christmas story as the husband of Mary and the stepfather of Jesus. The pious conception of him is that of an older man, a safe protector of Mary, a carpenter by trade, chaste and holy.

But what do we really know about him? When Mary became pregnant, Scripture says that Joseph, knowing the child was not his, decides to "divorce her quietly" to avoid a public inquiry that would leave her in an awkward and vulnerable situation. Then, after receiving a revelation in a dream, he agrees to take her home as his wife and to name the child as his own.

We understand that he spares Mary embarrassment, he names the child as his own, and he provides an accepted physical, social, and religious place for the boy to be born and raised. But he does something else that's not so obvious: He shows how a person can be a pious believer who is deeply faithful to everything within his religious tradition and yet at the same time open to a mystery beyond his human and religious understanding.

In essence, Joseph teaches us how to live in loving fidelity to all that we cling to as people of faith, even as we remain open to a mystery of God that takes us beyond all of our religious practices and our imagination. Isn't that one of the ongoing challenges of Christmas?

Joseph is open to a mystery beyond both his human and religious understanding.

Thursday
THIRD WEEK OF ADVENT

Revisiting the Visitation

In the biblical story of the visitation, Mary meets her cousin, Elizabeth. Both are pregnant. One carries Jesus, the other carries John the Baptist. The Gospels want us to recognize that both these pregnancies are biologically impossible. Mary's is a virginal conception, while Elizabeth conceives at an age far beyond a woman's normal childbearing years. So there's clearly something of the divine in each.

The Gospels present the children and their mothers to us as cousins. But the Gospels want us to think deeper than biology and family trees. They are cousins in the same way that Christ and those things that are also of the divine are cousins. And a curious thing happens when they meet. Christ's cousin, inside his mother, leaps for joy in the presence of Christ, and that reaction releases the Magnificat inside of the one carrying Jesus.

There's a lot in that image. Christian de Chergé, the Trappist abbot who was martyred in Algeria in 1996, suggests that, among other things, this image is the key to how we, as Christians, are meant to meet other religions in the world.

We need each other, everyone on this planet, Christians and non-Christians, Jews and Muslims, Protestants and Roman Catholics, Evangelicals and Unitarians, sincere agnostics and atheists. We need each other to understand God's revelation. Without the other, without recognizing that the other also is carrying the divine, we will be unable to truly release our own Magnificat.

Do we need to get to know other religions?

Friday
THIRD WEEK OF ADVENT

Mary Gives Voice to Human Finitude

Helplessness tugs at the heart. I am always touched in the softest place inside me by helplessness. Maybe you are, too. If so, we're in good company.

The good heart of Mary, the Mother of Jesus, moved her to go to her Son at the wedding feast of Cana and say: "They have no wine!" At one level, hers is a very particular request at a particular occasion in history. She is trying to save her hosts at a wedding from embarrassment, from suffering an indignity. But this incident has a deeper meaning. Mary is also speaking universally, as the mother of humanity, Eve, voicing for all of us what John Shea so aptly calls "the cries of finitude."

What is finitude? The finite, as we can see from the word itself, contrasts itself to the infinite, to what is not limited, to God. God, alone, is self-sufficient. God, alone, is never helpless. Everything else is finite. Thus, as humans, we're subject to helplessness, illness, lameness, blindness, hunger, tiredness, irritation, diminishment, and death. Our "wine" also will eventually run out. Hopefully someone like the Mother of Jesus will speak for us: *They have no wine!*

Recognizing and accepting our finitude should challenge us to hear more clearly the cries of finitude around us. Like Mary, we should take up the cause of those in need and ensure that someone spares them from indignity by changing their "water" into "wine"; for the helpless, we need to call out: *They have no wine!*

Let's open our hearts to the helpless.

Saturday
THIRD WEEK OF ADVENT

Mary's Courage and Example at the Cross

Sometimes, well-intentioned artists have painted Mary as lying prostrate under the cross, helplessly distraught, an object for sympathy. But such depictions don't honor what happened there nor teach the lesson of the cross. In this situation, prostration is weakness, collapse, hysteria, resignation. In the Gospels, "standing" is the opposite, a position of strength. Still, why the silence and why her seeming unwillingness to act or protest?

In essence, what Mary was doing under the cross was this: She couldn't stop the crucifixion, but she could stop some of the hatred, bitterness, jealousy, heartlessness, and anger that caused it and surrounded it by refusing to give it back in kind. She transformed rather than transmitted all that vile negativity by swallowing hard and eating bitterness rather than giving it back. Everyone else was doing that, but not the Mother of God.

Had Mary, in moral outrage, begun to scream hysterically, shout at those crucifying Jesus, or attacked the man who was driving the nails into Jesus, she would have been caught up in the same kind of energy affecting everyone else, replicating the very anger and bitterness that caused the crucifixion in the first place.

We need, at times, to protest, to shout, to throw ourselves into the face of injustice and do everything in our power to stop the "crucifixions" we see. But there are also times when darkness is going to have its hour and all we can do is to watch and wait under the cross. Like Mary, we must have the courage to say: "I can't stop this, but I will not perpetuate its hatred."

Why was Mary silent while her Son was crucified?

Fourth Sunday of Advent

For God so loved the world that he gave his only Son.

JOHN 3:16

The Checkered Origins of Christmas

If someone who had never heard the story of Jesus were to ask any of us about his origins, I suspect we would begin with the story of his annunciation and birth and end with the news of his resurrection and ascension. While those events and others capture his life, that's not how the Gospels either begin or end his story. The story of Jesus and the meaning of Christmas can only be fully understood by looking at where Jesus came from and by examining how his story has continued in history. Indeed, three of the four Gospels tell the story of Jesus by beginning with his family tree.

Mark's Gospel doesn't write about the family. He begins with Jesus' public ministry. The Gospel of John begins Jesus' story by pointing out his eternal origins inside of God before his birth. For John, Jesus' family tree has just three members: the Trinity. Matthew and Luke, however, include inside Jesus' story a long family tree, a genealogy that shows his origins. We may ignore this expansive list of difficult-to-pronounce names, most of which mean little to us. But as renowned biblical scholar Raymond Brown emphasizes, we can't fully understand the story of Jesus without understanding why his family tree, this vast list of names, is judged to be important.

What's to be learned from looking at Jesus' family tree, all those curious ancient names? Abraham fathered Isaac, Isaac fathered Jacob, Jacob fathered Judah…and so on. Among other things, these genealogies trace Jesus' origins in a way that tells us that his real story will not be grasped by anyone who wants to believe that Jesus' human origins were totally immaculate and pure, containing no sin or weakness.

Jesus wasn't born of all saintly ancestors. Rather, as the genealogies show, his family tree contains as many sinners as saints. Among his ancestors were sinners of every sort, including liars, adulterers, murderers, power-grabbing men, scheming women, wicked kings, and corrupt public officials. The same holds true for the religious institutions that figured in his birth. The religious history of Judaism out of which Jesus was born was also a mélange of grace and sin, of religious institutions serving both God and their own human interests.

What's the lesson in this? Both the people and the institutions that gave birth to Jesus were a mixture of grace and sin, a mixture that mediated God's favor and also rationalized it for its own benefit. But out of that amalgamation, Jesus was born. It can be a scandal to us to accept that not everything that gave birth to Christmas was immaculately conceived. The same holds true of what followed after Jesus' birth. His earthly ministry was also partially shaped and furthered by the self-interest of the religious authorities of his time, the resistance of secular powers of his time, and the fear and infidelity of his own disciples. Jesus' family tree subsequent to his birth is also a long list of saints and sinners, of selfless martyrs and selfish schemers, of virtue and betrayal.

Flawed persons and institutions were part of Jesus' original family tree, and they've been part of his Church ever since. Faith can accommodate the recognition of sin and infidelity. So can Christmas.

We can't understand the story of Jesus without knowing why his family is important.

Monday
FOURTH WEEK OF ADVENT

The Christmas Mystery as Cosmic

Perhaps the most neglected part of our understanding of Christ—though it's clearly taught in Scripture—is the notion that the mystery of Christ is larger than what we see visibly in the life of Jesus and in the life of the historical Christian churches. Christ is already part of physical creation itself.

We see this expressed, for example, in St. Paul's letter to the Colossians, where he writes of Christ: "He is the image of the invisible God, the firstborn of all creation. For in him were created all things in heaven and on earth, the visible and the invisible....All things were created through him and for him. He is before all things, and in him all things hold together" (Colossians 1:15–17).

Saint Paul's letter to the Romans tells us that just as people groan within our mortal limits and ache for immortality, so does all of physical creation. The earth also longs for salvation: "Creation awaits with eager expectation the revelation of the children of God. We know that all creation is groaning in labor pains even until now" and Christ will be its salvation (Romans 8:19, 22).

The mystery of Christ is more encompassing than what we can see visibly and historically. It also includes the notion that physical creation itself was somehow created through Christ, that Christ holds it together, and that Christ will give it an eternal future. The mystery of Christ is not just about saving us, the people on this planet, but also about saving the planet itself. The earth, too, should celebrate Christmas.

"All creation is groaning in labor pains."

ROMANS 8:22

Tuesday
FOURTH WEEK OF ADVENT

A Slow March to Goodness

God writes straight with crooked lines. That axiom sounds clever.
Can good ever arise out of evil? The answer to that question will
invariably be negative when we look at the surface of things. But faith is
never predicated on how things look on the surface. God's work is often
under the surface.

We see a poignant expression of this in a poem, *Meditation*, written
by Raïssa Maritain. The poem becomes more powerful as an expression
of faith when we know its background. This wasn't a simple expression
of faith in some abstract, dark time. The dark times were particularly
real to the poet.

In 1936, when she wrote this poem, Raïssa Maritain was witnessing
the ascent of Adolf Hitler and Nazism in Europe. Her world was
crumbling, her friends were dying, and she was scurrying for her
personal safety. Within that crushing context, she wrote this poem:

> Darkness from below, darkness from the heights;
> Beneath the Archangel's black wing
> The divine Plan unfolds.
>
> Infinite paradox of the creation:
> Eternity is being built with time,
> And good—imperishable—with evil's assistance.
>
> Mankind trudges along toward justice
> Through the lazy curves of iniquity,
> Today's error is at the service
> Of truth to come...

Today's error is at the service of tomorrow's truth. And so our
faith needs to look deeper than what's happening on the surface. God is
always alive and working underneath, even through our worst errors.

Hearing God's Heartbeat

The Last Supper account in John's Gospel gives a wonderful mystical image. John describes the beloved disciple as reclining on the breast of Jesus. What's contained in this image?

First, when you put your head upon someone else's chest you are able to hear his or her heartbeat. Hence, in John's image, we see the beloved disciple with his ear on Jesus' heart, hearing Jesus' heartbeat, and from that perspective looking out into the world. This is John's ultimate image for discipleship: The ideal disciple is the one who is attuned to Christ's heartbeat and sees the world with that sound in his or her ear.

Then there is a second level to the image: it is an icon of peace, a child at his mother's breast, contented, satiated, calm, free of tension, not wanting to be anywhere else. This is an image of primal intimacy, of symbiotic oneness, a connection deeper than romantic love.

And for John, it is also a eucharistic image. In this image we see a person with his ear on Jesus' heart, which is how John wants us to imagine ourselves when we are at Eucharist because, ultimately, the Eucharist is a physical reclining on the breast of Christ. In the Eucharist, Jesus gives us, physically, a breast to lean on, to nurture at, to feel safe and secure at, and a place from which to see the world.

The image in John's Gospel is a eucharistic one.

Thursday
FOURTH WEEK OF ADVENT

What Are We Looking For?

Some years ago, I went on a weeklong retreat where the retreat
director, Fr. Robert Michel, a French-Canadian Oblate missionary,
began the experience with these words: "I want to make this a very
simple retreat for you. I want to teach you how to pray in a particular
way. I want to teach you how to pray so that in your prayer, sometime,
perhaps not this week—perhaps not even this year, but sometime—you
will open yourself so that in your deepest self you will hear God say to
you, 'I love you!' Because before you hear this inside you, nothing will
be enough for you. Nothing will ever be quite right. After you hear
this from God, you will have substance. You will have found the thing
you've been seeking for so long."

The Gospel of John would agree with that. Near its end we read of
that poignant post-resurrection meeting between Jesus and Mary of
Magdala. Mary goes to the tomb on Easter Sunday morning wanting
to embalm Jesus' dead body. She meets Jesus but doesn't recognize him.
He says to her, "'Whom are you looking for?' She thought it was the
gardener and said to him, 'Sir, if you carried him away, tell me where
you laid him, and I will take him.' Jesus said to her, 'Mary'" (John
20:15–16a). Ultimately, all of us want the same thing: to hear Jesus call
our name in love.

Like Mary Magdalene, we want to hear the voice of God
speak one particular word.

A Birth Far Outside the City

God, it seems, favors the powerless, the unnoticed, children, babies, outsiders, and refugees with no resources and no place to go. That's why Jesus was born outside the city, in a stable, nondescript, outside all fanfare, and away from all the people and events that were deemed important at the time, humble and anonymous.

Scripture tells us that God's ways are not our ways and our ways are not God's ways. We tend to understand power by how it works in our world. There it works through popularity, through mass media, through historical privilege, through financial clout, through higher education, through idiosyncratic genius, and not infrequently, through raw aggression, greed, and insensitivity to the needs of others and of nature.

As Scripture shows, God works more through anonymity than through the headlines, more through the poor than the powerful, and more through those outside the circles of power than those inside them. When we examine how God works, we see it's no accident that Jesus was born outside the city and that after he was crucified, he was also buried outside the city.

On the surface, seeing power as residing in financial influence, political clout, charismatic talent, media influence, physical strength, athletic prowess, and attractiveness is not bad in itself. But looked at more deeply, as we see in the birth of Christ, God's word bypasses the centers of power and gestates instead in the hearts and consciences of those outside the city.

God's ways are not our ways.

December 24
CHRISTMAS EVE

Meaningful Anonymity

Most of us will live lives of quiet obscurity watching the big events of our world from the outside, always seeing someone other than ourselves as being at the center. It seems we will remain forever unknown, and our talents and contribution will not be recognized by anyone and find that the deep symphonies and melodies that live within us will never find satisfying expression in the outside world. Our dreams and our deepest riches will never find an earthly stage. It seems there will never be room in the inn for what is best within us.

Mary gave birth to the Christ in a stable because there was no room for them in the inn. This is a comment on more than just the busyness and inhospitality of some ancient innkeeper. It is a comment upon what lies deepest within human life.

In essence, what it says is that it is not those who sit at the center of things—the powerful, rich, or famous, government leaders, corporate heads, or scholars and academics—who ultimately sit at the center of life. What lies deepest and most meaningfully inside of life lies in anonymity, unnoticed and tenderly swaddled in faith.

What lies deepest within human life?

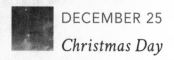

All this took place to fulfill what the Lord had said through the prophet: "Behold, the virgin shall be with child and bear a son, and they shall name him Emmanuel," which means "God is with us."

MATTHEW 1:22–23

The Present that Gives Forever

The fact that God incarnate is with us does not bring us immediate festive joy. Our world remains wounded; wars, selfishness, and bitterness linger. Our hearts also stay injured; pain persists. For a Christian, just as for everyone else, there will be incompleteness, illness, death, senseless hurt, broken dreams, cold, hunger, lonely days of bitterness, and a lifetime of inconsummation.

The Incarnation does not promise heaven on earth. It promises heaven in heaven. On earth, it promises us something else—God's presence in our lives. This presence redeems because knowing that God is with us is what ultimately empowers us to give up bitterness, to forgive, and to move beyond cynicism and bitterness. When God is with us, then pain and happiness are not mutually exclusive, and the agonies and riddles of life do not exclude deep meaning and deep joy.

We need to celebrate Christmas heartily. Maybe we won't feel the same excitement we once felt as children when we were excited about tinsel, lights, Christmas carols, special gifts, and special food. But something more important is still given to us, namely the sense that God is with us always, in our joys as well as in our shortcomings.

The word was made flesh. That's an incredible thing, something that *should* be celebrated with decorations and songs of joy. If we understand Christmas, then carols will flow naturally from our lips.

God's presence empowers us in many ways.

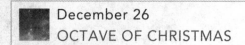
First, Remember the Good

I've never been happy with some of my activist friends who send out Christmas cards with messages like: "May the Peace of Christ Disturb You!" Can't we set aside one day a year to be happy and celebrate without having our already miserable selves shaken with more guilt?

Christmas is a time when God gives us permission to be happy, when the message from God speaks through the voice of Isaiah and says: "Comfort my people. Speak words of comfort!" Everywhere you look, you see heavy hearts. Moreover, many people are living with hurt and disappointment who don't see God and the Church as an answer to their pain but rather as somehow part of its cause.

So our churches, in preaching God's word, need first of all to assure the world of God's love, God's concern, and God's forgiveness. Before doing anything else, God's word is meant to comfort us—indeed, to be the ultimate source of all comfort. Only when the world knows God's consolation will it accept the concomitant challenge.

The peace of Christ, the message inside of Christ's birth, and the skewed circumstances of his birth, if understood, certainly disturb. May they also bring deep consolation.

In the celebrations of Christmas, speak words of comfort.

Watching with Our Hearts

"Shepherds [were] keeping the night watch over their flock"
(Luke 2:8). When the Gospel of Luke recounts the birth of our Lord, it
says that, when Jesus was born, shepherds were keeping watch in the
night. What were they watching for in the dark? They were looking
for much more than threats to their flocks. They were seeking light,
something to brighten their darkness.

John's Gospel doesn't give us a description of Mary and Joseph in a
stable at Bethlehem. Instead, the author uses an image to describe the
coming of Jesus. "Through him was life, and this life was the light of
the human race; the light shines in the darkness" (John 1:4–5). Notice
that John doesn't say that a light shines into the darkness; it shines *in* the
darkness. That's an important distinction.

Christmas speaks of childlikeness, wonder, innocence, joy, love,
forgiveness, family, community, and giving. When we're in touch with
these, we more easily see what's special inside of ordinary life. These
make light shine in the darkness.

Christmas asks us to imitate the shepherds, keep watch, and hope
to see light inside of darkness. When we're watching with our hearts,
there is more wonder than familiarity, more childlike trust than
cynicism, more love than indifference, more forgiveness than bitterness,
more joy in our innocence than in our sophistication, and more focus on
others than on ourselves.

Jesus is "the light of the human race."

JOHN 1:4

Bethlehem Inside Our Soul

To learn how to believe in Santa Claus again is one of the many challenges of Christmas. The challenge is not so much to return to the innocence of a child but to recognize that the knowledge and maturity we've gained from all our years of learning and experience is a necessary stage on the journey to a still deeper place.

That means it's not just important to learn and become sophisticated. It's equally important to eventually become post-sophisticated. It's not just important to grow in experience and shed naiveté, it's equally important to eventually find a certain "second naiveté." And it's not just a sign of intelligence and maturity to stop believing in Santa. It's a sign of even more intelligence and deeper maturity to start believing again.

Sometimes, seeing the innocence and youthful wonder in the eyes of our own children as they anticipate the celebration of Christmas can help us find a certain softness inside again—not at the same place where we once felt things when we were little and still believed in Santa but at a new place, a place beyond where we defined ourselves as grown up. That's the place where wisdom is born. That's also where Jesus is born. That's Bethlehem in the soul.

The celebration of Christmas can help us find a certain softness inside again.

Seeing the Church from Both Sides Now

Carlo Carretto was a monk who loved the Church deeply but wasn't blind to its faults and failures. He saw and proclaimed with disarming honesty that the Church, through its sin, can make it difficult for some to believe in God.

His deep love for his faith and his Church and his refusal to not turn a blind eye to the very real problems of the Church was an expression of a mature faith, one that wasn't so romantic and idealistic that it needed to be shielded from the darker side of things. His also was a faith that was real enough to avoid a cynicism that blinded a person to the evident goodness that also emanated from the Church.

In truth, the Church remains both horribly compromised and wonderfully grace-filled. Honest eyes and a mature heart can see and accept both. Many people have left the Church because it has scandalized them through its many sins, blind spots, defensiveness, self-serving nature, and arrogance. Many people wonder whether they can ever again trust the Church's structure, ministers, and authorities.

We *can* accept the Church despite its sin. Love and loyalty doesn't mean denying that sin exists. But it's important to see that the Church's many downsides never eclipse the superabundant, life-giving grace of God.

The Church is both horribly compromised and wonderfully grace-filled.

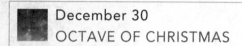

The Tiny, Most Powerful of Powers

God was born into this world as a helpless infant lying in the straw. That has huge implications for how we understand God's power and how we understand God's seeming silence in our lives.

Adam and Eve's primary motivation for eating the forbidden fruit was their desire to somehow grasp at divinity and possess Godlike power. Saint Paul shows us the antithesis of that when he writes that Jesus stayed fully divine and became fully human, emptying himself to become helpless, trusting that this emptying and helplessness ultimately would be the most transformative power of all.

That insight can shed light on how we understand what we might think is God's absence in our world. How might we comprehend what is often called the silence of God? Where was God during the Holocaust, the natural disasters that have killed people, and other tragedies?

God is present and intervenes in all situations, but not in the way we ordinarily understand. God is present in the way beauty is present, in the way a helpless, innocent newborn is present, and in the way truth as a moral agent is always present.

God is never silent because beauty, innocence, helplessness, and truth are never silent. They're always present, but unlike ordinary human power, they're present in a way that's completely nonmanipulative and fully respectful of your freedom. God's power, like that of a newborn, like the power of beauty itself, fully respects you.

How might we comprehend what is often called the silence of God?

God's Unimaginable Closeness

As Christians, we believe God is infinite and ineffable. This means that while we can know God, we can never imagine God. That truth makes it even harder for us to imagine that the infinite Creator of all things is intimately and personally present inside us, worrying with us, sharing our heartaches, and knowing our most guarded feelings.

Whenever we try to imagine God's person, our imaginations come up against the unimaginable. At this very minute, thousands of people are being born, thousands are dying, thousands are sinning, thousands are acting virtuously, thousands are making love, thousands are experiencing violence, thousands are feeling their hearts swell with joy.

How can one heart, one mind, one person be consciously on top of all of this and so fully aware and empathetic that no hair falls from our heads or sparrow from the sky without this person taking notice? It's impossible to imagine, and that's part of the very definition of God.

How can God be as close to us as we are to ourselves? That's part of the mystery and wisdom bidding us to befriend mystery, because anything we can understand is not very deep! The mystery of God's intimate, personal presence inside us is beyond our imaginations. While God is infinite and ineffable, God also is very close to us, closer than we imagine.

We can be filled with joy that God keeps up with all of us.

The LORD bless you and keep you! The LORD let his face shine upon you, and be gracious to you! The LORD look upon you kindly and give you peace!

NUMBERS 6:24–26

A New Year's Resolution

What might be a good New Year's resolution?

In a wonderful little book, *Biography of Silence*, Pablo d'Ors of Spain stares his mortality right between the eyes and decides this is what he wants to do in the face of the inalienable fact that he's going to die one day:

"I have decided to stand up and open my eyes. I have decided to eat and drink in moderation, to sleep as necessary, to write only what contributes toward improving those who read me, to abstain from greed, and never compare myself to others. I have also decided to water my plants and care for an animal. I will visit the sick, I will converse with the lonely, and I will not let much time go by before playing with a child. In the same manner I have decided to recite my prayers every day, to bow several times before the things I consider sacred, to celebrate the Eucharist, to listen to the Word, to break bread and share the wine, to give peace, to sing in unison. And to go for walks, which I find essential. And to light the fire, which is also essential. And to shop without hurry, to greet my neighbors even when I do not like seeing their faces, to subscribe to a newspaper, to regularly call my friends and siblings on the phone. And to take excursions, swim in the sea at least once a year, and to read only good books, or reread those that I have liked."

I'm a two-time cancer survivor. When the cancer returned the second time, the doctor told me, in unequivocal terms, that my time was probably short. No more endless days. That prognosis clarified my thoughts and feelings as nothing ever before. Stunned, I went home, sat down in prayer, and then wrote my own creed. It's also the prayer with which I opened this booklet:

I am going to strive to be productive for as long as I can.

I am going to make every day and every activity as precious and enjoyable as possible.

I am going to strive to be as gracious, warm, and charitable as possible.

I am going to strive to be healthy as long as I can.

I am going to strive to accept others' love in a deeper way than I have up to now.

I am going to strive to live a more fully "reconciled" life. No room for past hurts anymore.

I am going to strive to keep my sense of humor intact.

I am going to strive to be as courageous and brave as I can.

I am going to strive, always, to never look on what I am losing but rather to look at how wonderful and full my life has been and is.

And I am going to, daily, lay all of this at God's feet through prayer. Amen.

Life has never been more precious, nor more enjoyable. Not incidentally, since writing that prayer I have also begun to water plants, care for a feral cat, and feed all the neighborhood birds.

When Jesus was born in Bethlehem of Judea, in the days of King Herod, behold, magi from the east arrived in Jerusalem, saying, "Where is the newborn king of the Jews? We saw his star at its rising and have come to do him homage."

MATTHEW 2:1–2

The Contrasts of Christmas

Inside the Christmas story are a number of smaller narratives, each very rich. One is the story of the three Wise Men. We see this richness in the Gospel of Matthew where the writer sets up a powerful contrast between the reaction of the Wise Men and King Herod to the birth of Jesus.

We're all familiar with this story since it has been much celebrated in song, icon, and legend. Jesus' birth is announced to the faith community by the angels, by supernatural revelation. But for those outside of that faith tradition, his birth is announced to them through nature, through the stars. The Wise Men see a special star appear in the sky and begin to follow it, not knowing where or to what it will lead.

While following the star, they meet King Herod who, upon learning that a new king supposedly has been born, has his own evil interest in mind. He tells the Wise Men to find the child and bring him back information so that he, too, can go and worship the newborn. We know the rest of story.

The Wise Men follow the star, find the new king and, upon seeing him, place their gifts at his feet. What happens to them afterward? We have all kinds of apocryphal stories about their journey back home, but these, while interesting, are not helpful. We don't know what happened to them afterward, and that is exactly the point. Their slipping away into anonymity is a crucial part of their gift. The idea is that they now disappear because they *can* now disappear. They've placed their gifts at the feet of the young king and can now leave everything safely in his hands. Like old Simeon, they can happily exit the stage singing: Now,

Lord, you can dismiss your servants! We can die! We're in safe hands!

And Herod, how much to the contrary! The news that a new king has been born threatens him at his core since he's a king. The glory and light that will now shine upon the new king will no longer shine on him. So what is his reaction? Far from placing his resources at the feet of the new king, he sets out to kill him. Moreover, to ensure that his murderers find him, he kills all the male babies in the entire area.

What's the lesson for us? Can we bless new life that threatens us? Like the Wise Men, can we lay our gifts at the feet of the young and move toward anonymity and eventual death, content that the world is in good hands, even though those hands are not our hands? Or, like Herod, do we try somehow to kill that life?

To bless another person is to give away some of one's own life so that the other might have more resources for his or her journey. Good parents do that for their children, good teachers for their students, good mentors for their protégés, good pastors for their parishioners, good politicians for all the people they serve, and good elders for the young. The Wise Men did that for Jesus.

How do we react when a young star's rising begins to eclipse our own light? With blessing or curse?

The Wise Men follow the star,
find the new king and place
their gifts at his feet.
And then?

...on Scripture, literature,
...sonal experience, Fr. Ron
...er shows God's love in
...abundance that our souls
...n for that love. God lies
...de us as an invitation that
...ly respects our freedom, never
overpowering us, never leaving us.
God-as-invitation, precisely like
a baby lying in the straw, gently
beckons us, but he's helpless.
God can't make us pick up and
accept his invitation.

For each day of Advent and
through the octave of Christmas,
Daybreaks invites you to pray
and reflect on the coming of the
Messiah, the word made flesh.

"For God so loved the world that he gave his only Son."

JOHN 3:16

RON ROLHEISER, OMI,
is an internationally
renowned spiritual
author, speaker, and
community builder. He
has a master's degree in theology
from the University of San Francisco,
and a PhD and an SThD from the
University of Louvain, Belgium. Fr.
Ron is a member of the Missionary
Oblates of Mary Immaculate and is
president of the Oblate School of
Theology in San Antonio.

Liguori
PUBLICATIONS
A Redemptorist Ministry

ISBN 978-0-7648-2819-5

9 0 0 0 0>

9 780764 828195